FOUR
steps to
▲▲▲▲▲▲▲▲▲▲
DYNAMIC PREACHING

ROBERT PAGLIARI, C.SS.R., Ph.D.

LIGUORI
PUBLICATIONS

One Liguori Drive
Liguori, MO 63057-9999
(314) 464-2500

Imprimi Potest:
James Shea, C.SS.R.
Provincial, St. Louis Province
The Redemptorists

Imprimatur:
+ Edward J. O'Donnell, D.D.
Archdiocesan Administrator, Archdiocese of St. Louis

ISBN 0-89243-525-9
Library of Congress Catalog Card Number: 93-78616

Cover and interior art by Chris Sharp

CONTENTS

DEDICATION

To Mike Huber
for teaching me to be patient and
to think positively through the ups and downs
of the golf course, and for being patient
with me while I was thinking conceptually
through the sand traps and
water hazards of life;

To his father, Dennis,
a man with the ability to empty
a sleeve of new golf balls
off the first tee into a lake, smile, say,
"God, I love this game," and refer to the
entire experience as sanity maintenance;

To his mother, Marielena,
a woman with the ability to worry constantly
because she loves unconditionally.

ACKNOWLEDGMENTS

My sincere thanks to these kind people who read the manuscript and offered helpful suggestions:

Beth Vandergrift
Doug Cook
Gene Sylva
Dave Mellot

PROLOGUE

A Directive From Saint Alphonus Liguori Regarding Preaching

...Speak in a simple style. Carefully avoid in your sermons...every pretentious and affected word. Let all that you say be familiar and comprehensible. We should always choose language that is most intelligible to the hearers, and not high-flown words...which [are] not clear. Employ only the language that is usual and is adapted to the intelligence of all classes of people...and your sermons will be productive. [Speak] in a natural manner. When in the pulpit we should speak as if we were addressing several persons assembled in an apartment, entertaining them on some virtue or relating to them some event. Thereby...the happiest results are produced.

Brother Alphonso
Letter 743
to Father Luigi Capuano

INTRODUCTION

R obots can't thumb their noses. My brother— who leaves the remote-control unit for his TV on the coffee table—found this out for himself only recently. Far be it from me to suggest that my brother is lazy, but one day he told me he wished somebody would invent a robot that would go to the coffee table, pick up the remote-control unit, and hand it to him. That way he wouldn't have to lean forward to pick it up from the table himself. But inventing a mechanical hand that has the same dexterity as a human hand is no easy task. Robots don't have thumbs. Well, not as efficient as ours anyway. Not yet.

Television producers love people like my brother. They want folks to sit back and stay tuned to one channel—their channel. They try hard to begin prime-time viewing with a popular show because, once people select a station, inertia sets in and they usually won't change to another station, no matter how bad the programs become. Why do people sit in front of the tube and watch programs of poor quality? Is it inertia? Is it because they're lazy? Or is it because they're hopeful? Maybe they're hoping that the *next* program will be better or the *next* episode will be interesting or the *next* movie will be engaging.

I find this fascinating. Night after night, week after week, year after year, people sit in front of the tube hoping that the programs will get better. True, cable brought in more variety, but most programs have not improved.

Still, people keep watching, listening, waiting, and hoping. I wonder sometimes. Are they in a rut? Are they in a "hoping habit," ritually coming back hoping that the next time will be better? But the next time isn't any better. Still, they keep coming back. I don't understand why. Maybe they don't have anything better to do. Are they mere robots?

There's something else I don't understand. People go to church on Sunday expecting to hear a good sermon, but they rarely do. Most sermons are filled with boring content. And the way the sermon is preached is boring, too. But people keep coming back Sunday after Sunday. Why? Is it because they're hopeful? Are they hoping that maybe the *next* sermon will be better or interesting or engaging?

I find this fascinating. Sunday after Sunday, week after week, year after year, people sit in church hoping that the sermons will get better. True, Vatican II brought in more variety, but the sermons have not improved. Are the Sunday churchgoers like the nightly TV watchers?

I've heard some pretty lousy sermons in my time. I've given my share, too. But people, like mechanical beings, just keep coming back.

People keep watching, listening, waiting, and hoping. Are they in a rut? Are they in a "hoping habit," ritually coming back hoping that the next time will be better? But the next time isn't any better. Still, they keep coming back. Maybe they don't have anything better to do. I think if I were a listener instead of a preacher and I had to sit through lousy sermons every week, I'd *find* something better to do.

I don't like ruts and I don't like robots. It bothers me when preaching and preachers fall into a rut of mediocrity. It concerns me when people file mechanically into church, sit and stare into space, cough frequently, read the bulletin, clip their fingernails, examine their watches, and leave when the service is over feeling relieved because it's over.

I do like good preaching. I like it when people enjoy coming to church because they're looking forward to hearing good preaching. It may be that preachers who do not preach effectively or dynamically have forgotten the primary purpose of the homily.

The homily derives its purpose from the core message of Christianity: conversion—turning away from what is wrong and toward what is right. Therefore, the purpose of a homily is to convert people; to move people away from wrong behavior and toward right behavior, from doubt to faith.

Since the primary purpose of the homily is conversion, the preacher must be knowledgeable about three aspects of the listeners.

1) The PEOPLE being moved,
2) Where they're being moved FROM,
3) Where they're being moved TO.

Without this knowledge, it is impossible to deliver an effective homily.

What does *effective* mean? It means that the item in question can accomplish the purpose for which it was intended. A can opener is effective when it is able to open cans. Otherwise it is ineffective, or broken. A homily is effective when it moves people. If it does not move people, then it is ineffective. We know that a homily has been effective when, as a result of their listening to the homily, people change their attitudes or behaviors in such a way that they move *away* from being less Christian and *toward* being more Christian.

The purpose of this book is to provide a method for creating an effective homily. This method includes both the content of the homily (what is said) and the delivery of the homily (how it is said). When both the content and the delivery of a homily have accomplished a change in attitudes or behaviors, then, and only then, has effective and dynamic preaching occurred.

If you want to improve your preaching effectiveness, you will find this book helpful. If you don't want to improve your preaching effectiveness, then I presume that you have something better to do at the moment. That's fine. But let me make one suggestion. Leave this book on your coffee table in front of the television. Who knows? Some evening, after handing you the remote-control unit, the robot may not be interested in watching TV and might want to thumb through this book instead.

Oh, I forgot. Robots don't have thumbs. Or do they?

NOTES

step 1
▲▲▲▲▲▲▲

SHARPEN YOUR PERCEPTION

I f you want to improve your preaching, the best way to start is to sharpen your perception. Good preaching requires good perception. Let's review the difference between *observation* and *perception*. Observation involves the use of one of the senses. Perception is the interpretation of what you observe. Observation is a matter of external behavior. Perception is a phenomenon that happens internally. Perception is the process by which your brain attaches meaning to your observation.

Here's an example that distinguishes observation from perception. Suppose you walked into a room and saw a man crying. You might think to yourself, *Gee, poor fellow. I guess he must be feeling really sad.*

Maybe he received some bad news just before I walked into the room.

What did you observe? A crying man. What did you perceive? That he was feeling sad.

We will assume that what you saw was accurate: a man with tears rolling down his face, a crying man. We can make this assumption because it is rarely our sight that is deceived. More often it is our perception that gets fooled.

Your perception—that the crying man was feeling sad—may or may not be accurate. Your brain is in the habit of taking what it sees and bringing meaning to it. In the past, when you saw people crying, they were usually feeling upset and sad. Now, whenever you see a person crying, your brain almost automatically brings the same internal meaning, the same perception, to this external behavior. However, your perception may not be accurate this time.

Let's say you decide to ask the man, "What's wrong? Why are you crying?" If he says, "I just got some bad news," then your perception was accurate. The internal meaning (he's feeling sad), which your brain attached to what you saw externally (a man crying), was a correct match.

However, it is also possible that your perception was an incorrect match. When you asked, "What's wrong? Why are you crying?" the man could have replied, "There's nothing wrong. I'm crying because I'm so happy. I just found out that I won the state lottery!" In this case, what you *observed* was correct: a crying man. But what you *perceived* was totally incorrect. The man was not feeling sad. On the contrary, he was feeling very happy.

Good preaching, then, is a matter of good perception, accurate perception, correct perception. This clarity of perception must be brought to bear in three different arenas: the values esteemed by the congregation (the PEOPLE being moved), society's values (what they're being moved FROM), and the values put forth by Scripture (what they're being moved TO). Your homily, and the manner in which you deliver it, will become more effective as your perception approaches closer to a correct match between each of these arenas and their respective values.

A practical sequence to use as you prepare the content of an effective homily is to begin with the Scripture arena (what you're moving the people TO), then to look at the congregation arena (who are the PEOPLE you're trying to move), and then to examine the society arena (what you're moving the people FROM). In each step you are attempting to sharpen your perception about the values espoused by each arena.

NOTES

step 2
▲▲▲▲▲▲▲

IDENTIFY THE VALUES IN THE ARENA OF SCRIPTURE

T he first arena that requires good perception is the Scripture arena. An effective and dynamic preacher must have an accurate perception of the Bible. Commentaries on the Bible—both the Old Testament and the New Testament—abound. Numerous volumes have been published that describe the historical context, the socioeconomic background, and the language nuances of the Scriptures. It is possible to investigate a single verse, a chapter, or an entire book of the Bible. Likewise, you can explore a theme, a recurring phrase, or a particular character in as much depth as you have the energy, resources, and time to put into such an endeavor. You should immerse yourself as completely as you can into the particular verse or verses of Scripture that you will be using in your homily. In the pulpit, you will use only about one fifth of what you know about a particular passage. This does not mean that the other four fifths of your research is in vain. On the contrary, having this "extra" knowledge is what will give you confidence to speak with dynamic enthusiasm and to proclaim the Good News with authority.

Is this study step really necessary? Yes, it is. If you have a calling to preach God's word then it is your responsibility to investigate the Bible; to immerse yourself as completely as possible into a clear understanding of God's word. Since you cannot give what you don't have, you must be knowledgeable about the word that has been entrusted to you to speak to others.

When you complete your investigation of the Scripture passage, you will perceive a transcendental goal, a Christian virtue, a gospel value, that is contained in that passage. This is the mark of the first arena and can be characterized as a hallmark. It is a truth revealed by God; a goal set forth from the heart of the divine Creator that attracts the heart of the human creature.

If you can write down in one complete sentence, the goal, the hallmark, the gospel value that is revealed in this particular Bible passage, then you have completed the second step toward more effective preaching. You have gained a clear perception of the Scripture arena.

example
▲▲▲▲▲

Here's an example from the parable of the Good Samaritan: We should go out of our way to help people in need even at considerable expense and inconvenience to ourselves.

NOTES

step 3

▲▲▲▲▲▲▲

IDENTIFY THE VALUES IN THE ARENA OF YOUR CONGREGATION

T he second arena that requires good perception is the congregation; not just any congregation, but *your* congregation. What is your perception of the people who sit in front of you? Who are these people who come to listen to you preach? This is not merely a matter of memorizing their names or keeping records of their weekly offering. Knowing these two variables will not make your preaching effective.

What you must endeavor to perceive about the people in the pews is not their identity or how much money they make but, rather, the values that they ascribe to. This is the perception that you must ascertain about them. Granted, it is information that is far more subtle than finding out their street address or income bracket. But it is, nevertheless, information that you can obtain.

How will you obtain this information? What questions will help you perceive your congregation's values? Many of their values are the result of their common, public histories. The influences, messages, and experiences of the past have shaped the values they hold at the present time. Therefore, one way to discover many of their values is to ask historical questions.

- What were they taught to value most at home and in school?
- What were they taught to value least?
- Which behaviors were acceptable when they were youngsters?
- Which behaviors were not acceptable?
- Who were their heroes?
- What values did their heroes represent?
- How did they spend their leisure time?
- How did they spend their money?
- What background information would most characterize them or least characterize them?
- What values were popular when the majority of them were growing up?

- What messages constituted the American dream, a successful occupation, a wholesome relationship, a happy life?
- What historical or global events occurred that would have affected their lives and values significantly? For example, what wars, economic conditions, natural disasters, dreaded diseases, medical breakthroughs, technological inventions, aerospace accomplishments, and national or international struggles and successes made up their histories?
- In what way have these phenomena shaped your congregation's values?

Questions like these will help you perceive what kind of people they are today.

Let's look at another example.

example
▲▲▲▲▲

Comic-book characters like Superman and Wonder Woman went out of their way to help people in distress.

An effective preacher cannot be content with a facile answer as regards the congregation's values. If you come to the conclusion that these people are "good" people, then you haven't the foggiest idea about them or their values. Any congregation of people gathered in any church in the world can be characterized as "good" people. You have to know *these* people. You have to have an accurate perception of their fears and hopes, their disappointments and dreams, their failures and strengths, their struggles and accomplishments.

If you know what would make these people laugh or cry, or what would make them happy or sad, then you probably have a correct perception of their histories and of the values they were taught in the past.

Your knowledge of what they were taught to value constitutes a "watermark" for this particular congregation. Why a watermark? Consider the trees that grow along the shore of a body of water. During a dry season, these trees bear a mark, a dark line on their trunks, indicating where the water level used to be. The values of the people in your congregation can be compared to the watermark on a tree. In times of plenty, when rain is abundant, the water level is maintained. So, too, with the support of an encouraging homily, your congregation's values maintain their optimum level, the established watermark. Conversely, in times of drought the water level falls. In time of distress and confusion, people tend to doubt, reconsider, or at least, reprioritize their values. This is rarely a preferred situation any more than a prolonged drought or a scorching heat wave is a preferred situation.

Two forces work to lower the established watermark of your congregation's values. The first is a significant negative emotional experience. This is usually very personal and, therefore, beyond the scope of this discussion. The second force is the appeal of an opposite set of values. This is a gradual decline brought about by the lure of those societal values that lie in direct opposition to the gospel values. The goal of an effective preacher is to continually reinforce and support the Christian values that are already present in the congregation. Effective preaching will maintain the watermark of their optimum values and move people away from the scorching yet alluring heat of a competing set of values—society's values.

NOTES

step 4
▲▲▲▲▲▲▲

IDENTIFY
THE VALUES
IN THE ARENA
OF SOCIETY

H ow do you develop a clear perception of society's values? Interestingly enough you can focus once again on your congregation. But this time, instead of asking historical questions, you can ask contemporary questions. If you ask questions regarding specific experiences that they are having now, you will gain an immediate perception of what these people are struggling against and an accurate perception of society's values. Here is a sampling of contemporary, as opposed to historical, questions that can give you a start.

- What events, values, and messages are occurring now that are affecting these people in their day-to-day lives?
- What is the current quality of life for them?
- What is the quality of the environment in which they live and work?
- How long does the average marriage last?
- How much money do they spend per month on groceries, transportation, housing, and other living expenses?
- What ads are they being bombarded with?
- What music is most popular and what values do the lyrics of this music suggest?
- What television shows, movies, and videos are the current box-office hits and what values do these films promote?
- What news items or magazine articles have they read during the past week?
- What mass-media messages are they subjected to in the course of their workweek, and what are the underlying values in these messages?

These specific experiences are most significant because they are most immediate. From one Sunday homily to the next, it is paramount that you, as preacher, be acutely aware of the messages that these people receive. It is even more important that you gain a clear perception of the values that underlie these messages.

From movies to manufacturing, billboards to bumper stickers, T-shirts to telemarketing, society declares which behaviors are acceptable and which products are desirable. In doing so, society establishes its own mark for people to live up to—or down to. By comparison to the hallmark of Scripture's values, society's values actually "miss the mark," an Old Testament phrase, which means "sin."

example
▲▲▲▲▲

Here's an example of the negative impact of society: If you see someone in distress, don't get involved.

Take just a cursory glance through the daily newspaper of any metropolitan city and you're bound to find samples of what society values. Progress is preferred to people. Expansion excels over the environment. Youthfulness attracts and aging repels. Infidelity is acceptable. Might makes right. Crime not only pays, it pays well. And the golden rule remains: Whoever has the gold makes the rules!

Values are not only present in news items but also promoted in advertisements: Buy this, buy that; here's the latest fashion; here's the best sale; buy, buy, buy; having *more* is always *better*. People are continually reminded that no matter how satisfied they are with the product they're using, there's a "new and improved" version available, and they must go out and buy it *now*!

As your perception becomes sharper, you will begin to appreciate just how divergent society's values are from the Scriptures' values. This shouldn't surprise you since consumerism is based on selfishness and the gospel is based on selflessness. However, it does clearly define the task of the preacher and the measure of an effective homily.

The task of the preacher is to move the congregation away from the missed mark of society, beyond the watermark of their personal histories and closer to the hallmark of Christianity. The measure of an effective homily is the extent to which the congregation demonstrates this change—away from selfishness and toward selflessness. Your responsibility is to relate the three arenas in such a way that your congregation can clearly recognize the truth of Scriptures' values and the illusion of society's values.

NOTES

step 5

▲▲▲▲▲▲▲

RELATE THE THREE ARENAS

A t this point you have gained a clearer perception of the Scriptures' values (what you want to move the people TO), of your congregation's values (the PEOPLE you're attempting to move), and of society's values (what you want to move them FROM). Now it is your task to relate these three arenas to one another. Relating these three arenas is easily accomplished by thinking in terms of comparison or contrast. Keep in mind that when you relate the three arenas by comparison, your homily will function in a supportive way. Your intention must be to reinforce an attitude or behavior that is already present and is consistent with the Christian message. When you relate the three arenas by contrast, your homily will function in a persuasive way. Your intention must be to change an attitude or behavior that is present but is clearly inconsistent with the Christian message.

COMPARISON

Here's an example of how the three arenas can be related by comparison. The key is to find a similar thread that is common to all three.

1. *The Scripture arena.* We will assume that the Scripture passage is the parable of the Good Samaritan. The value espoused here is that true Christians go out of their way to help people in need, even at considerable expense and inconvenience to themselves.

2. *The congregation arena.* The people in your congregation were taught the value of helping others while they were growing up. In your homily, you can give a personal example to demonstrate this. Simply ask, "How many times have your parents told you to go out of your way to help someone else?" or "How many of you can remember seeing your parents go out of their way to help someone in need?"

3. *The society arena.* You won't have any difficulty finding a contemporary illustration of this value in the news since the press regularly reports stories of civil servants who save people in distress. In your homily, you can ask, "How many of you noticed the article in last Thursday's paper about the firefighter who rescued a child from the burning building on Sixth Avenue?"

Now you've connected the three arenas by comparison. You did this by underscoring the value of helping others that is apparent in each. So your homily will function in a supportive way to reinforce this Christian behavior.

An effective preacher might conclude as follows: "The value of helping someone else is a value that Christ spoke about in the gospel parable. It is a value that our parents instilled in us while we were growing up. It is a value that we see some people in our society demonstrating today, as in the case of this firefighter's successful rescue. The 'considerable expense' that firefighters demonstrate is their willingness to risk their lives to help others. I would like to congratulate all of you for the times that you have gone out of your way to help others, for the times that you've demonstrated the helping behavior that should be associated with all true Christians. You may not have been terribly inconvenienced or been called upon to risk your life. You didn't make the front page of the daily news. And maybe nobody knows about it but you and the person you helped—the blind person you directed across the street, the missionary in India you sent a dollar to. But God knows about it. And God rewards us accordingly. All of us have the responsibility to engage in such behaviors, as our parents did, for the sake of being good models to our children and all young Christians who look to us for good example. This is how we were brought up in the Faith. And this is what it means to bring up others in the Faith. This is how we all continue to be good Samaritans to one another."

CONTRAST

Here's an example of how the three arenas can be related to one another by contrast. The key is to find a point of departure or conflict. Since the point of conflict will ordinarily occur in the society arena, we can begin by relating the Scripture arena and the congregation arena to each other by comparison as demonstrated above.

1. *The Scripture arena.* Once again we will assume that the Scripture passage is the parable of the Good Samaritan and that the value being espoused is helping other people in need.

2. *The congregation arena.* We will assume that the people in your congregation are familiar with the most famous comic-book heroes. In your homily, you can compare these two arenas by saying, "The parable of the Good Samaritan reminds us to go out of our way to help people in distress. Remember, when we were growing up, how excited we would get when Superman or Wonder Woman would help someone in distress? We wanted to be just like them, heroes to the rescue of the weak and the disadvantaged."

3. *The society arena.* To contrast the first two arenas with the society arena, we might discover a news article that demonstrates a lack of concern for people who need help. For example, consider a story about several people who witness a street crime—a purse snatching or a beating—but do nothing to intervene. They don't want to get involved. They don't want to be bothered. They fear repercussion. They are reluctant to give testimony to the truth. They elect to peer out of their windows and watch, but they choose not to help.

An effective preacher might conclude like this: "Is this what we've come to today? It's a far cry from two thousand years ago. A far cry from what Christ taught us. A far cry from the comic books of childhood. We must be involved in our faith; we must give actions to our faith. To be silent is to imitate the Pharisees—hypocrites. They say they believe, but they do nothing to lighten others' burdens.

"Christ knew of our temptation to apathy and fear. He said, 'Let this cup pass from me; yet not as I will, but thy will be done.' And it was God's will that Christ get involved. When he stood before Pilate, when he came to Calvary, he didn't say 'I don't want to get involved. I don't want to be bothered. I'm afraid of the repercussions. I won't testify to the truth.' On the contrary, Christ became so involved that he died for the sake of the truth, for our sake, for our sins. Are we so apathetic now that Christ would have to return again, to die again? Would we say, 'If Jesus wants to get involved, fine. But I'm not.'

"Perhaps Christ has become just another comic-book figure for you, a childhood hero that you've outgrown. Perhaps his involvement in your salvation does not move you anymore. Well, if Christ can't convince you to get involved, and Superman and Wonder Woman can't convince you to get involved, then *I* certainly can't convince you to get involved. Of course, you may feel differently when the day comes that *you* are the victim in this newspaper account. When you are the woman whose purse is stolen or you are the elderly man who is beaten and robbed. Then, when you look around at the faces in the windows, when you see people watching you being hurt and you wonder why they won't get involved, look very closely at those faces in the windows. You'll see your own face staring back at you and saying, 'I don't want to be bothered. I don't want to get involved. I will not testify to the truth. I will not help you.' "

NOTES

step 6

▲▲▲▲▲▲▲

REFLECT, MEDITATE, AND PRAY

A s they prepare their Sunday sermons, some preachers choose to begin with this step. Others choose to conclude with it. Placed here, it may appear to be a "middle" step. But *reflect, meditate, and pray* is actually an ongoing and integral part of the entire preparation process. Reflection is less of a step and more of a stance that underlies all of the other steps. Meditation and prayer establish a communion between God and the preacher, which cannot be neglected.

If you disconnect yourself from prayer and meditation, you will distance yourself from the very *Subject* of your sermons. If your preparation is without reflection, your preaching will be worthless. A parrot would be equal to the task.

Are you a preacher or a parrot? The people in your congregation will be moved more by *who* you are than by *what* you say or by *how* you say it. Authenticity is the foundation of effective preaching.

Christ once indicated to his listeners that if they could not put their faith in him, they should put their faith in his actions. Put another way, if they didn't believe because of what he *said*, they should believe because of what he *did*. What he did was a reflection of who he was.

Even two thousand years ago people realized that talk is cheap. They needed demonstrations, actions that gave credibility to words. So Christ gave them actions to accompany his words. In this way, he established a hallmark for all the preachers who would come after him. What people *say* is not as clear a reflection of who they *are* as what they *do*. If you aren't what you say you are, if you yourself don't *do* what you tell others to do, you are a hypocrite. And if you are a hypocrite, you have no business preaching to others. Prayer rescues us from hypocrisy. Prayer brings us into contact with humility because it reminds us of our humanity. To pray is to assume the position of the creature in the presence of the Creator. To pray is to remind ourselves that all power and all authority come from God. God gives life to our words because God gives meaning to our words. God entrusts to our words the divine power, authority, life, and meaning of his Word. Preaching is the incarnation of the present moment. Through our words, the Word is born again. In this sense, every preacher can be thought of as a life-bearing, life-giving person, and every preaching event can be thought of as Christmas!

In prayer, preachers come to realize that they have been entrusted with an awesome gift and a most profound responsibility: to speak about God. They must attempt to understand God, to live and move and have their being in God, to direct the overwhelming energy, which is God's love, into the hearts of people in such a way that those people respond in kind and in love, to God and to one another.

A preacher who rises from prayer and enters a pulpit without trembling at the thought of this responsibility has not prayed. A preacher who speaks without any fear is a gifted orator, a skillful technician, a clever actor, or a colorful parrot, but not really a preacher.

Reflection, meditation, and prayer will bring you into contact with the chaos that exists in society, in the congregation, and in yourself. Silent reflection is a process that is frequently avoided because it hurts. Resist the temptation to avoid this process. Meditating is a cleansing fire that burns but does not destroy. Praying will not give you the right to preach to others, but rather the humility to preach to others.

Without this step you can talk all you like, but you will not move anyone because your words will not ring true. The people may be polite enough to listen to you, but they will not be foolish enough to believe you.

Reflection, meditation, and prayer will also bring you into contact with the harmony of God's word. Just as effective preaching moves people closer to Christ, effective praying moves the preacher closer to the people. Reflection, meditation, and prayer will help you to care about your congregation. What motivates a preacher to preach is concern for the people in the pews. If you don't care about the people you serve, you can be quite content with mediocre preaching—halfhearted "homilettes," which will produce little more than halfhearted "Christianettes."

NOTES

step 7
▲▲▲▲▲▲▲

CHOOSE A FAMILIAR SYMBOL

I am always amazed at how little credit we give to Christ. He was an extremely effective preacher. He left us a clear blueprint to follow, but most preachers don't follow it. Christ continually used visual images when he spoke. He used familiar visual images: bread, wine, vine, branches, seeds, wheat, salt, fish, coins, sparrows, flowers, and the hairs on our heads. There was a dual advantage in using ordinary images. The point of his message was more clearly understood because he appealed to the eyes, not just the ears, of his listeners. And the message was easily recalled each time the listeners encountered the symbol again—each time they baked bread, each time they harvested wheat, each time they combed their hair.

So why do so many preachers today use words alone and no visual images? Is it valid to assume that people today are more verbally attuned and less visually attuned than people were two thousand years ago? I don't think so. On the contrary, there are more video stores opening around town than there are libraries being built. Book sales are not likely to overtake cinema profits in the near future. If anything, we're becoming more visually oriented, not less. Music discs are accompanied by video tracks. Telephones have become televiewers. The dashboards of our cars are virtual panoramas of screen plots, diagrams, and graphic displays.

Why have preachers remained verbal and verbose when the congregation is more visually sensitive than ever? A picture is not worth a thousand words today; it's worth four times that amount. As a result, you should choose a familiar symbol that captures the message of your homily and use it.

Speaking of visual images, have you found yourself looking forward to seeing the robot associated with each step? A robot is not a flattering symbol for the people in a congregation or for a preacher. It's more of a counter symbol actually—stiff, rigid, unemotional....

NOTES

step 8

▲▲▲▲▲▲▲

SHOP FOR A SPRINGBOARD

P oems are filled with visual imagery. But listening to a poem that describes a flickering candle flame is a different experience than actually watching a candle flame flicker while the poem is being recited. The second scenario leaves less to the imagination, but generally leaves a longer lasting impression.

Preachers can use visual imagery when they speak or they can reinforce their words with physical objects. Here's an example of the difference between the two. I can say, "Listen to this quote from last Thursday's newspaper," and then read the quote to the congregation from my notes. Or I can bring the newspaper with me into the pulpit, hold it up, and say, "This is last

Thursday's paper. Now listen to this..." and actually read the lines from the paper instead of just talking about them. The second instance makes a stronger impression on the congregation because it's more dynamic and engaging. Effective preachers learn to become comfortable in handling physical objects that complement what they're saying.

When you read the homily excerpts in step five, what were some of the visual images that came to mind? Did your mind's eye picture a bright red firefighter's helmet? Did you recall the classic pictures of Superman and Wonder Woman that are prominent on the front covers of those comic books?

Wouldn't the delivery of such a homily have a much greater impact if the preacher actually displayed a firefighter's helmet or a classic comic book? Absolutely!

Think of all the physical objects that already exist in the church where you preach. When was the last time you pointed to the altar or the cross or the Bible while you were giving a sermon? Those are obvious symbols. What about some others—communion wafers, wine, water, candles, pews, baptismal font, stations, Easter candle, collection plates, pillars, windows, lights, musical instruments, hymnals, flowers, carpets, colors, textures, the pulpit itself? There are, right in front of you, physical objects that you can easily point out to enhance your message.

There are even more physical objects available in and around the rectory, many that occur in the gospels. Bread, salt, oil, jars, grapes, figs, honey, fruit, coins, seeds, stones, sticks, weeds, thorns, keys, and cloth are right at your fingertips, readily available, and free.

If a visual referent is not already available in church, in the rectory, or on the grounds, go out and shop for the item. Discount stores are a preacher's delight. Under one roof you can find a visual reinforcement for just about any homily idea imaginable. And they're reasonably priced!

How many homilies and sermons have you listened to in your life? How many of them can you recall? Not many, right? To this day, I receive letters from former parishioners who recall a Christmas homily I preached over six years ago. I handed out a strand of tinsel to everyone in the congregation. I paid $4.99 for a box of one thousand strands. Isn't this a small price to pay? The congregation can remember the point of the homily—as tinsel reflects the light from the Christmas tree so we are called to reflect the light of Christ to one another—years later. Talk about a priceless return on an economical investment!

If you don't reinforce the point of your homily with a physical object, most people won't remember what you said beyond twenty-four hours. Some won't remember what you said beyond the parking lot as they drive away.

Look for and shop around for a simple object that captures the message, or at least part of the message, of your words. Learn to become comfortable in handling such physical objects in the pulpit. You will be amazed at the lasting impression that visual techniques have on your visually sensitive congregation.

NOTES

step 9
▲▲▲▲▲▲▲▲

OPEN WITH A BANG

N ever, ever begin by saying, "Today is the Tenth Sunday in Ordinary Time." Whereas the most important sentence that comes out of a preacher's mouth is the *last* sentence of the homily, the second most important is the opening sentence. You must capture your congregation's attention immediately. If you don't, you've lost a significant opportunity that can never be regained. Preachers who have the notion that they must "work into" their homilies, who start out slowly and then "warm up" their listeners, will end up having to "wake up" their listeners instead.

What are some examples of riveting ways to begin a homily?

1. Ask a rhetorical question.
2. Ask a nonrhetorical question.
3. Use a short anecdote.
4. Share a personal story.
5. Tell a humorous, albeit relevant, joke.
6. Read a quote.
7. Deliver a memorized quote.
8. Use a line of poetry.
9. Recite a lyric from a song.
10. Repeat a familiar ad.
11. Sing a familiar jingle.
12. Use body language.

These twelve suggestions do not constitute an exhaustive list of attention-getting ways to begin a homily. But they already provide three months of engaging openers—and without repetition!

I enjoy preaching. I've discovered that there's a direct, positive correlation between how much I enjoy preaching and how much people enjoy listening to me. If I'm feeling "down," not as prepared as I should be, or feeling ill on a given Sunday, I don't enjoy preaching as much. And I hear about it in no uncertain terms. If I'm "up," especially well prepared and eager to jump into the saddle, I really enjoy preaching. I pull out all the stops and I'm positive that this will be my best homily yet. I hear about that, too. There must be a communication loop that is set in motion between the preacher and the congregation. The initial "charge" that sets this loop in motion has to come from the preacher. If the preacher initiates this communication cycle with a bolt of enthusiasm, the congregation responds and returns a larger bolt of enthusiasm to the preacher. This further "energizes" the preacher who sends more enthusiasm back to the congregation and so on. The loop becomes more and more "electrical," and the turnaround time quicker and quicker, to the point where the cycle is so great and so rapid that communication becomes communion.

But remember, the only way to set this dynamic and effective communication loop in motion is to open with a bang.

NOTES

▲▲▲▲▲▲▲▲▲

IDENTIFY WITH THE PEOPLE

"**I**f you're going out, make sure you have clean underwear on. You never know when you might be in an accident and have to be taken to the hospital." All of the adults that I've met claim that these were their mother's parting words as they left through the front door. How universal is this? When I worked in Belgium, the secretary, who was born and raised in Holland, told me that her mother said the very same thing to her when she was growing up. The quote has become so universal that I suspect many adults would swear their mothers said it even if they hadn't. Whether or not every mother has decreed the warning is immaterial. The point is that it captures a host of motherly experiences: caretaking, pride, mild accusation, loyalty, good breeding, unsolicited advice giving, cradling, worrying, grooming habits, conscience formation, hovering, suspicion, caution, personal hygiene, respect, love, and just a dash of guilt for good measure.

Everyone can identify with these motherly experiences. Preachers who key into examples that are part of their congregation's experiences will establish a solid bond with the listeners. When you can identify with the people in this way, many of them will start nodding their heads affirmatively. This means that they identify with you. They can relate to what you just said. They understand you. They agree with you.

Whether you realize it or not, identification will lead to the promotion of five major phenomena.

1. *Affinity.* This means that people will perceive themselves as having more in common with you as a result of the identification process. They will realize, consciously or unconsciously, "This preacher is more like me than I thought. We have a lot in common."

2. *Attraction.* This means that people will like you. They will think, "Now this is the kind of preacher I would like to have for a friend, someone I would like to invite over for dinner some evening."

3. *Credibility*. This means that people will believe you. "Now here's someone who has expertise—knows what they're talkin' about, someone I can put my faith in, someone I can believe in."

4. *Trustworthiness*. This may not mean your congregation would follow your advice in banking investments or that they would buy a used car from you. But they would give you more than the benefit of the doubt when you speak on spiritual matters. They would see you as honest, someone who would not lie to them.

5. *Reciprocal comprehension*. This is an especially gratifying phenomenon. It means not only that the congregation understands the preacher but also that the preacher is perceived as an understanding person. "At last, someone who understands what I'm going through." This is quite therapeutic and compelling. "Now there's someone I could talk to if I ever get into trouble.

The identification process is obviously a potent one. Identification paves the way to change, to moving the listeners from non-Christian behavior to Christian behavior. The moral imperative here is that the preacher is bound not to abuse this step.

Preachers who cannot or who choose not to identify with the congregation remove themselves from the affinity, attraction, credibility, trustworthiness, and comprehension of the congregation. These preachers are untouchable and unable to touch the hearts of their listeners. Instead of speaking words that demonstrate how they themselves are participating in the struggles, hopes, fears, and joys of life, their words betray their observer role. They are standoffish. Their words are cold walls, isolating the congregation from God and from one another when their words should be building firm bridges connecting the congregation to God and to one another.

By insulating themselves from identifying with the people, these preachers also cast the Church and its teachings into a medieval castle, surrounded by an unbreachable moat. They severely limit the welcoming words that Christ speaks through the Church. If your words tell the people that you don't identify with them, they will know that your help and your heart is unavailable to them as well.

NOTES

step 11

▲▲▲▲▲▲▲▲▲

STICK TO
ONE POINT

I f a pollster stood outside your church after Sunday services and asked the members of your congregation to state the point of your sermon in one sentence, what would the results be? Before your listeners can summarize the point of your homily in one sentence, *you* must be able to summarize the point of your homily in one sentence.

We can learn a lesson from advertising. Manufacturers of consumer products spend millions of dollars on advertising each year. Television commercials cost tens of thousands of dollars to produce and hundreds of thousands to broadcast. Advertising firms are in the business of helping other businesses sell merchandise or services. National commercials are slick,

dynamic, and effective. They have to be. They have only a few seconds to convince consumers to buy a product. Here's an example: Brush with Glowbrite toothpaste, the one used by dentists—the *experts* in dental care.

Preachers can learn an important lesson from these advertisers. Preachers should be able to summarize the main point they want to communicate in one sentence.

Unfortunately, many preachers have the false idea that they have to use their homily time to explain the meaning of the Bible in great detail. This is simply not true. You should never allow your homily to become a short course in scriptural exegesis. If you feel a need to give a detailed explanation of each verse of the Scripture readings and all of the psalms proclaimed on Sunday morning, then consider starting a Bible-study group. There are people who want to know the details of the Bible and who will be happy to come and listen to you lecture on an evening during the week. But most people do not come to church on Sunday morning to listen to lectures. They come to be moved. Their goal is to make it through the coming week. What they need to hear from you is that God knows they're trying hard, God loves them, and God calls them to draw closer by entering more deeply into holiness. Your homily, then, is a vehicle for God's understanding, compassion, and inviting motivation.

example

▲▲▲▲▲

As we discussed earlier from the parable of the Good Samaritan, the one point of the homily is: God calls Christians to help people in trouble. The three arenas—Scripture, congregation, and society—provide the fertile ground from which to draw examples which reinforce this single point. The concept was proclaimed in the Scripture, practiced during our childhood years, but is blatantly denied in today's society. So what are you going to do about it?

The explanations of the Scripture arena, the identifications in the congregation arena, and the contrasts in the society arena are different value perspectives of the same point. But the idea is always clear and concise because it boils down to one point—going out of our way to help someone else who is in trouble.

I received a lovely call one afternoon. A woman in the parish phoned to say her family had been entertaining guests the night before and the topic of church came up. A nonpracticing guest made the mistake of challenging her nine-year-old son to recall a sermon he had heard in church. Much to his mother's pride, the boy unhesitatingly recounted the dramatic interpretation of the "suntanned Thessalonians" about which I had preached the previous Sunday.

"But what really amazed me," the mother concluded, "and that's why I had to call and tell you, is that my son *understood* the point you were making: Don't sit around like a beach bum waiting for the Second Coming of Christ when you can get up and make the kingdom of heaven come alive by doing something Christian right now."

I'm happy to report that the nonpracticing friend of these parishioners began to show up regularly at our church services. Such is the power of sticking to one point!

NOTES

step 12

▲▲▲▲▲▲▲▲▲

CLOSE WITH
A PUNCH

T his is a tough one. The last sentence of a homily is the most strategic position of all. The last sentence has the potential of being remembered the longest. The last sentence has the potential of being the most forceful. The last sentence also has the potential of short-circuiting all the work that went before it!

You have probably heard (or made) comments like "I wish Deacon Smith wouldn't repeat himself." This comment really means that Deacon Smith doesn't know how to exit. He doesn't know when to stop. He doesn't know how to close with a punch so he goes back and preaches his homily all over again.

Unless you're deliberately saying the same words

over and over for the sake of emphasis, don't repeat yourself. This is deadly. Never end with a summary. "And so, to reiterate...." This is deadly. Never talk about stopping. "Now in conclusion let me say...." Just stop. But stop with a punch. Otherwise this is deadly. And stop using this tired excuse as a substitute for a punch, "So as we continue our prayer together today, let's keep in mind what we heard...." This is weak and should be laid to rest.

Two sentences that all preachers should be able to deliver from memory are the first sentence and the last sentence of their homilies. If you forget everything else in between, say the first sentence and the last and sit down! It may be the shortest homily you've ever given, but it won't be the least effective.

Too many good preachers don't do their own homilies justice because they "wimp out" just before the round is over. Talk about trading in a potential first place gold medal and settling for last place. This is sad.

How do you end with a punch? The challenging twist-with-a-punch-in-a-series-of-mirrored-rhetorical-questions is at the top of my list.

example

What are you going to do about it? Are you going to join the ranks of the silent, unthinking, uninvolved non-Christians? Or will you think, speak, and act like Christ would today?

The twist is the monosyllabic words *think, speak,* and *act* in the last sentence after saying *silent, unthinking,* and *uninvolved* in the sentence before. The punch occurs when the people hear these words coupled with *non-Christian* and *Christ*, respectively. This ending is just challenging enough to be remembered and just uncomfortable enough, just "punchy" enough, to move them.

NOTES

step 13

▲▲▲▲▲▲▲▲▲

PREPARE AND REHEARSE

C ured for life! That was the result of my
Wallingford experience. I was newly ordained—
a baby priest. I was to preach my very first
parish mission in a church in Wallingford, Connecti-
cut. Talk about being overprepared. That was me. I
had the entire week of sermons written and memorized. I had all of my visual aids lined up and ready. I
prayed until my knees hurt. I was determined that this
mission was going to be the most successful experience of conversion that had ever hit this sleepy New
England town. I was so prepared, so ready to charge
ahead, that I decided I didn't need to rehearse. That
was a fatal mistake.

The first evening came. The church was packed. I walked deliberately into the sanctuary and then into the pulpit: a high, marble-coated, recently refurbished, carpeted, spacious, well-lit pedestal, a befitting monument for an enthusiastic upstart (who was about to bury himself).

I stood up tall and listened to my voice float into the state-of-the-art microphone and out of the perfectly balanced speakers. *Yes,* I thought to myself as I spoke, "a microphone system that is worthy of a great preacher." I ignored the little voice in my head that whispered something about pride going before the fall. I was not about to fall. I *had* these people. I had them in the palm of my hand. I could see it in their faces. They were hanging on every word I said.

Then I came to an emotional point. I leaned forward so that I could speak the dramatic line in a perfectly hushed voice. I knew I needed to be closer to the microphone to achieve the desired effect. As I leaned forward on my toes the microphone died. I had to shout the sentence that should have been delivered in a whisper. I thought, *No problem. They'll have this microphone fixed for tomorrow's service. Just keep up the volume so you can fill this church.* I leaned back on my heels and shouted the next sentence just as the microphone kicked in again. The result was a vocal blast that made me shiver and left the people holding their hands over their ears.

Well, it's working again, I thought. I decided to try another whispered effect. I leaned forward and the amplification system died again. Just what I needed on my first mission: a system on the blink!

I finished the sermon through the on-again off-again vacillations of technology and left the pulpit frustrated and furious. I was not going to put up with this inferior equipment for a whole week. I marched into the pastor's study.

I asked, "Did you hear my talk tonight?"

He said, "Yes."

"Well? Are you going to have the microphone fixed?"

"It's not broken," he replied.

I asked, "What do you mean?"

"It's not the microphone," he explained. "It's you! You keep moving back and forth. You have to stand still in that pulpit because there's a switch underneath the rug that's sensitive to weight. Each time you lean forward you're taking your weight off you heels, and that triggers the switch and shuts the microphone down automatically. Didn't anyone ever teach you to get familiar with the church you'll be preaching in before you open your mouth?"

I learned an important lesson in Wallingford: it's not enough to practice what you preach, you have to practice *where* you preach. Never, ever underestimate the detrimental effects that the environment can have on you and your preaching. Take the time to test the amplification system beforehand. Make sure that batteries are fully charged, lights are operational, and mechanical devices are in good working order.

If you are going to use a portable visual aid during your homily, always rehearse with it. Place it where it cannot be seen until you refer to it, and return it to where it cannot be seen when you're finished with it.

While you're preparing your homily, keep in mind that what you write is destined to be heard, not read. Your thoughts need not be literary masterpieces for the eye but memorable conversation for the ear. An effective homily may read poorly, but will sound rich. An effective homily derives its richness from the sincere reflection of faith, holiness, conviction, and concern presented in a conversational style. Saint Paul wrote this about preaching: "Say only the good things people need to hear, things that will really help them." An effective homily must be delivered and heard as a conversation between two friends. If a member of the congregation says, "I felt like you were talking directly to me," then you can be sure that many others felt the same way. You can be sure that your delivery style is personable and clear. You can be sure that your content is on target for these people.

Before you rehearse, know your material and know your congregation. If you believe strongly in what you're saying, you won't need to bring notes or even an outline with you into the pulpit. If you're used to having notes in front of you when you preach, the prospect of not having them may sound frightening. But you'll be amazed at the difference in the preaching experience. You'll be amazed also at the response from your congregation. Once you experience the authenticity, freedom, and dynamism that comes from preaching without notes, once you experience the intimacy that develops between you and the people, you will never be able to return to reading your homilies again. Reading your homilies would be settling for less. You won't want to settle for less, and the congregation won't let you settle for less.

Effective and dynamic preaching requires a great deal of preparation and rehearsal time. Preachers who spend less than twenty hours preparing a Sunday homily are cheating themselves, robbing their congregation, and insulting the Word of God. If you're too busy to spend twenty hours preparing and rehearsing your homily, then you're too busy—trying to do too much.

I once told a vice president of AT&T that I think some preachers spend too much time talking about money and not enough time talking about compassion. He told me I'm right. He was certain that if preachers spent more time talking about compassion they'd never have to talk about money, because their collection plates would always be full. "The laborer is worthy of pay" assumes that the laborer is working hard in the Lord's service. To be an effective and dynamic preacher you must work diligently in the Lord's service and in service to others. You must be committed, conscientious, and caring enough to prepare and rehearse. What you say must come from your heart. How you say it must come from your lips and reflect what is in your heart. Both content and delivery require your time and attention. When content is well prepared and delivery is well rehearsed, your labors in the Lord's service and in the service of others will yield a rich harvest.

NOTES

step 14

▲▲▲▲▲▲▲▲▲

SOLICIT HONEST FEEDBACK

O ne way to determine whether your preaching is effective now is to ask for feedback from your regular listeners. Through a form submitted anonymously, your listeners' reactions can be very helpful.

Here's an easy way to sample some feedback. Go to a stationery store and buy a box of thirty-two legal-sized envelopes. Go to the post office and buy thirty-two stamps. Make thirty-two copies of the Preaching Feedback Sheet that follows and place one form into each of the envelopes. Write your name and address and place a stamp on each envelope. Count out four envelopes and put a rubber band around them. Continue to sort the envelopes until you have a total of eight 4-packs. Give the stack of eight 4-packs to a competent parishioner and explain that you want these 4-packs distributed to eight people in the congregation. The people selected should be from a variety of ages and backgrounds.

For the two months that follow this distribution process you'll receive some honest feedback about your preaching. Take it to heart because it comes from the heart. You'll get responses from people who care about you and who want to see you become a more effective and dynamic preacher so that they can be moved to becoming more effective and dynamic Christians.

Preaching Feedback Sheet

I'd like to improve my preaching effectiveness. You can help. The feedback form in each envelope you received is the same. Please fill out one form each Sunday for the next four weeks, or every other week if you prefer. You can begin this week or wait until next week, but please return all four envelopes to me over the next two months. Thank you for your willingness to help evaluate my preaching.

DATE: _____

1. The main point of the homily was...

2. One thing I liked about what I heard was...

3. One thing I liked about how it was said was...

4. My biggest difficulty with the preaching is...

5. A topic that would help me is...

Age:

under 21   21-30   31-40   41-50   51-60   61+

CONCLUSION

Father Jones was old when I entered the seminary. I once heard a confrere say that Father Jones was older than dirt. He wasn't that old, of course, but he did predate the copy machine. Whenever he wanted a duplicate of something, he'd slip a piece of carbon paper into his typewriter. We'd tease him and ask why he didn't use the photocopier. He'd say, "You can't teach an old dog new tricks." We'd humor him and let him ramble on about the good old days. But every once in a while he'd make a trip to the main office and pretend to be busy searching through the storage cabinets. In fact, he was observing the copy machine. He was leery of and maybe even a bit frightened by this high-powered technology. But he was also fascinated by it. He marveled at the speed and precision of the machine. He knew it was a cost-effective, time-saving addition to the office. But he stood his ground just the same. "You can't teach an old dog new tricks," he'd mutter again as he walked out the door with a fresh supply of carbon paper. Father Jones was not going to give in, no matter how fascinating the new technology might be.

Then one day his attitude changed. He overheard two students complaining that they couldn't read the notes he handed out in class. The third and fourth carbon copies weren't as clear as the original. The students wanted to do well in his course and were interested in the material, but they were becoming frustrated by his antiquated methods of disseminating information. They were even thinking of dropping the course and enrolling in another professor's class. They didn't want to do that, but they didn't have much of a choice. At least the other professor's notes would be more legible.

That was all Father Jones needed to hear. His whole life was dedicated to his students. His entire identity was grounded in their education. His greatest satisfaction was in seeing them grow beyond their limits and meeting greater and greater challenges. His concern for the people he loved and served was enough to motivate him to switch from carbon paper to photocopies.

I don't know much about old dogs and new tricks. Maybe concern for others makes the tricks seem less difficult to perform. Maybe love for others enables the people doing the loving to feel, well, not so old.

Father Jones was willing to change. His motivation for changing was based on concern for others. What a tragedy it would have been if he hadn't cared enough to change for the sake of his students, if he had been content to stand by and watch them hitch a ride to another class, to thumb their way away.